INCONSEQUENTIAL DILEMMAS

KNOCK KNOCK®

VENICE, CALIFORNIA

Created and published by Knock Knock
1635-B Electric Avenue
Venice, CA 90291
knockknockstuff.com

ISBN: 978-160106486-8
UPC: 825703-50014-1

TABLE OF CONTENTS

INTRODUCTION

If you're looking for love or planning to switch careers, you'll find a host of helpful books to guide your decision-making process. But what of those less momentous choices we face on an hourly basis—for example, *How should I procrastinate? Should I squish this bug?*

These sorts of questions may seem relatively minor, but they comprise the bulk of the decision making we perform every day—and, thus, the bulk of the choices we make over the course of a lifetime. Who's to say what their cumulative impact may be? How do we know that these small reckonings, apparently so trivial in the short term, are less influential in the long run than the "biggies"?

We don't.

And so to be on the safe side, we've created *Inconsequential Dilemmas*, a collection of flowcharts to help you navigate those minor close calls with systematic confidence, ensuring a lifetime of sound choices and peace of mind.

Researchers date the term "flow chart" to around 1920, when early industrial-efficiency experts began using flowcharts to map manufacturing and other business systems. Most likely, however, flowcharts go back much farther, and probably sprang from mathematics. Some credit the first flowchart to Ada Lovelace, who in 1843 composed an algorithm that is now considered the world's first computer code.

In today's digital era, flowcharts have become one of the most popular forms of Internet meme. Whether you're an egghead or airhead, you can enjoy these charts' capacity to illuminate problems in their entirety, both as linear processes and holistic systems. Like engineers of the early 20th century, we remain enchanted by the form's ability to help us visualize and deal with the unpredictability of life. All around us is chaos, yet flowcharts give us a sense of structure. Thanks to their satisfying lines and boxes, we may not only make better decisions in our careers, but also in our Halloween costumes, haircuts, and karaoke selections.

I DROPPED FOOD ON THE FLOOR.

Can I Eat It?

7

IS THIS LOOK BOHO OR HOBO?

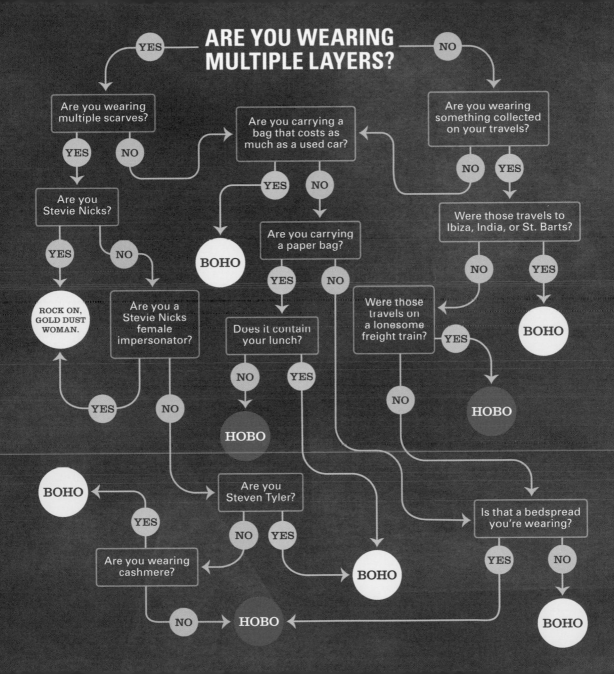

ARE YOU WEARING MULTIPLE LAYERS?

YES

NO

Are you wearing multiple scarves?

YES NO

Are you carrying a bag that costs as much as a used car?

Are you wearing something collected on your travels?

NO YES

Are you Stevie Nicks?

YES NO

YES NO

BOHO

Are you carrying a paper bag?

Were those travels to Ibiza, India, or St. Barts?

ROCK ON, GOLD DUST WOMAN.

Are you a Stevie Nicks female impersonator?

YES NO

Does it contain your lunch?

NO YES

Were those travels on a lonesome freight train?

YES

NO YES

BOHO

YES

NO

YES

HOBO

YES

NO

BOHO

HOBO

HOBO

BOHO

Are you Steven Tyler?

NO YES

Is that a bedspread you're wearing?

YES

Are you wearing cashmere?

NO YES

YES NO

BOHO

NO

HOBO

BOHO

I CAN'T SWEAR WITH THESE FREAKING KIDS AROUND.

––––––––

WHAT SHOULD I SAY INSTEAD?

DID YOU DROP YOUR PHONE IN THE TOILET?

NO · YES ----------→ FRAGGLE ROCK

Did you spit-take Guinness all over your shirt?

RUGGER BUGGER ←------- YES · NO

Did you serve Syrah in champagne flutes?

NO · YES ----------→ SACRÉ BLEU

Did another prospector jump your claim?

DAGNABBIT ←------- YES · NO

Did you get the computer sad face?

NO · YES ----------→ When did you last save?

Did some landlubber replace the rum with water?

BLISTERING
BARNACLES ←------- YES · NO

A few minutes ago · An hour ago

Did someone talk smack behind your back?

NO · YES ----------→ BOLSHEVIK

FUDGE · HOLY SHIFT KEY

Did a superhero foil your dastardly plans?

CURSES ←------- YES · NO

Did you make poor "Reply All" choices?

NO · YES ----------→ Did your boss get it?

Did some whoreson stab you with his rapier?

NO · YES

ZOUNDS ←------- YES · NO

SON OF A
BISCUIT · MELON–FARMING
SHEEP FLOCKER

RATS.

11

I left my reusable 👜 in the 🚗. Do I go back and get it?

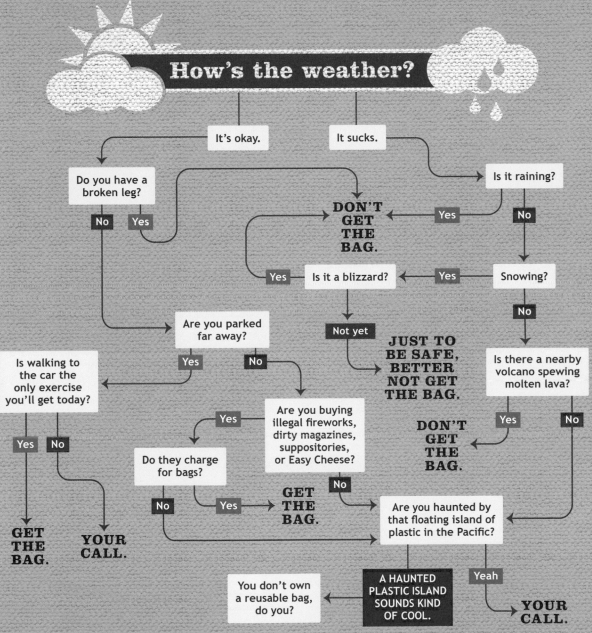

How's the weather?

It's okay. | It sucks.

Do you have a broken leg?

No | Yes

Is it raining?

Yes → DON'T GET THE BAG.

No

Snowing?

Yes → Is it a blizzard? ← Yes

No

Is it a blizzard? → Yes → DON'T GET THE BAG.

Not yet → JUST TO BE SAFE, BETTER NOT GET THE BAG.

Are you parked far away?

Yes | No

Is walking to the car the only exercise you'll get today?

Yes | No

Are you buying illegal fireworks, dirty magazines, suppositories, or Easy Cheese?

Yes | No

Is there a nearby volcano spewing molten lava?

Yes → DON'T GET THE BAG. | No

Do they charge for bags?

No | Yes → GET THE BAG.

GET THE BAG. | YOUR CALL.

Are you haunted by that floating island of plastic in the Pacific?

A HAUNTED PLASTIC ISLAND SOUNDS KIND OF COOL. → You don't own a reusable bag, do you?

Yeah → YOUR CALL.

Am I

TOO OLD

TO BE AT THIS PARTY?

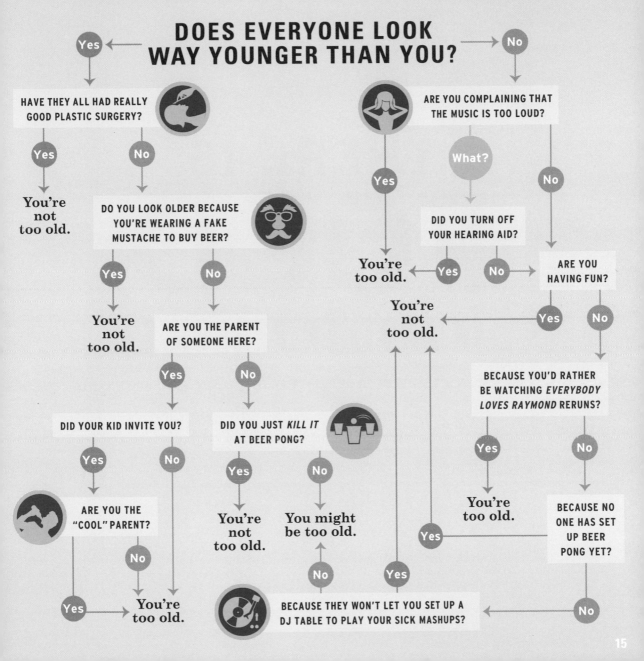

DOES EVERYONE LOOK WAY YOUNGER THAN YOU?

Yes ← → **No**

HAVE THEY ALL HAD REALLY GOOD PLASTIC SURGERY?

Yes → You're not too old.

No → **DO YOU LOOK OLDER BECAUSE YOU'RE WEARING A FAKE MUSTACHE TO BUY BEER?**

Yes → You're not too old.

No → **ARE YOU THE PARENT OF SOMEONE HERE?**

Yes → **DID YOUR KID INVITE YOU?**

Yes → **ARE YOU THE "COOL" PARENT?**

Yes → You're too old.

No → You're too old.

No → **DID YOU JUST KILL IT AT BEER PONG?**

Yes → You're not too old.

No → You might be too old.

ARE YOU COMPLAINING THAT THE MUSIC IS TOO LOUD?

Yes → You're too old.

What? → **DID YOU TURN OFF YOUR HEARING AID?**

Yes → You're too old.

No → **ARE YOU HAVING FUN?**

No → **ARE YOU HAVING FUN?**

Yes → You're not too old.

No → **BECAUSE YOU'D RATHER BE WATCHING EVERYBODY LOVES RAYMOND RERUNS?**

Yes → You're too old.

No → **BECAUSE NO ONE HAS SET UP BEER PONG YET?**

Yes → You're not too old.

No → **BECAUSE THEY WON'T LET YOU SET UP A DJ TABLE TO PLAY YOUR SICK MASHUPS?**

Yes → You're not too old.

No → You might be too old.

THERE IS
FOOD
IN ANOTHER PERSON'S
TEETH.

DO I SAY SOMETHING?

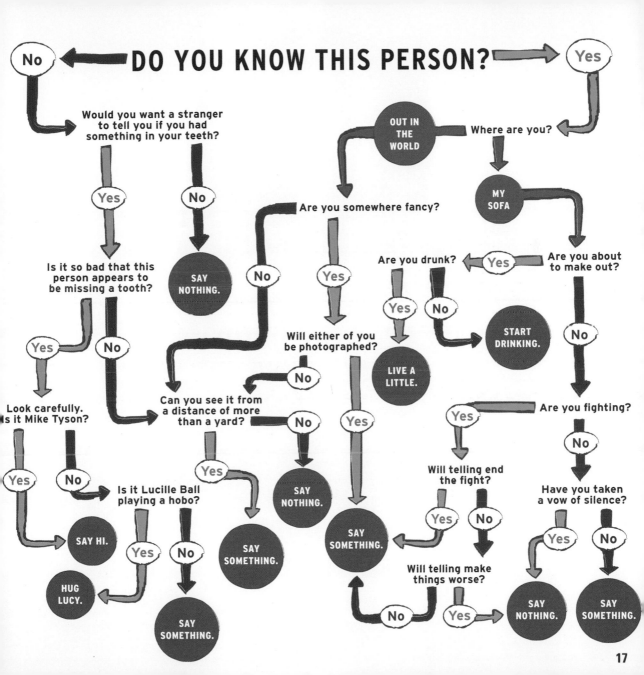

MAYBE
I LEFT THE DOOR
UNLOCKED.

I COULD HAVE
LEFT THE DOOR
UNLOCKED.

SHOULD
I GO BACK
AND CHECK?

HAVE YOU CHECKED AT LEAST ONCE ALREADY?

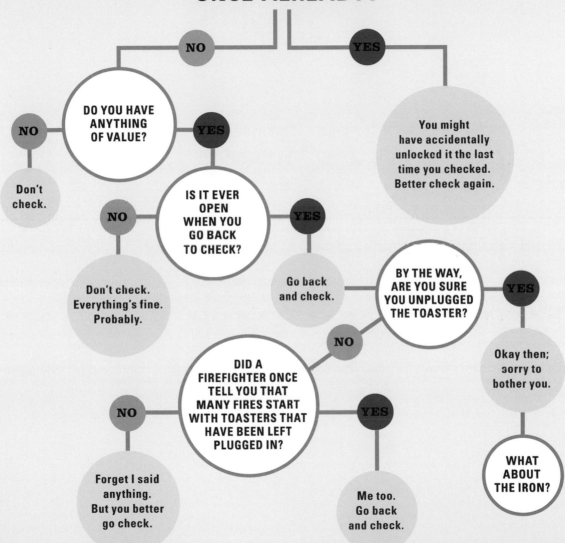

NO / **YES**

NO — **DO YOU HAVE ANYTHING OF VALUE?** — **YES**

Don't check.

YES — You might have accidentally unlocked it the last time you checked. Better check again.

IS IT EVER OPEN WHEN YOU GO BACK TO CHECK?

NO — Don't check. Everything's fine. Probably.

YES — Go back and check.

BY THE WAY, ARE YOU SURE YOU UNPLUGGED THE TOASTER? — **YES**

NO

Okay then; sorry to bother you.

DID A FIREFIGHTER ONCE TELL YOU THAT MANY FIRES START WITH TOASTERS THAT HAVE BEEN LEFT PLUGGED IN?

NO — Forget I said anything. But you better go check.

YES — Me too. Go back and check.

WHAT ABOUT THE IRON?

SHOULD I GO TO

LAW SCHOOL OR START A ROCK BAND?

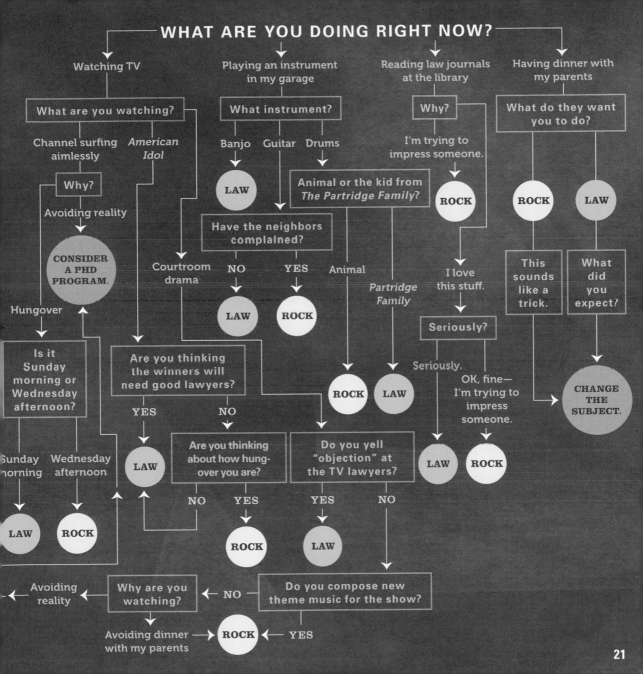

WHAT ARE YOU DOING RIGHT NOW?

Watching TV

What are you watching?

- Channel surfing aimlessly
  - Why?
    - Avoiding reality → **CONSIDER A PHD PROGRAM.**
  - Hungover → Is it Sunday morning or Wednesday afternoon?
    - Sunday morning → **LAW**
    - Wednesday afternoon → **ROCK**
- *American Idol*
  - Are you thinking the winners will need good lawyers?
    - YES → **LAW**
    - NO → Are you thinking about how hungover you are?
      - NO → **ROCK**
      - YES → **LAW**
- Courtroom drama → Do you yell "objection" at the TV lawyers?
  - YES → **LAW**
  - NO → Do you compose new theme music for the show?
    - YES → **ROCK**
    - NO → Why are you watching?
      - Avoiding reality →
      - Avoiding dinner with my parents → **ROCK**

Playing an instrument in my garage

What instrument?

- Banjo → **LAW**
- Guitar → Have the neighbors complained?
  - NO → **LAW**
  - YES → **ROCK**
- Drums → Animal or the kid from *The Partridge Family*?
  - Animal → **ROCK**
  - *Partridge Family* → **LAW**

Reading law journals at the library

Why?

- I'm trying to impress someone. → **ROCK**
- I love this stuff.
  - Seriously?
    - Seriously. → **LAW**
    - OK, fine— I'm trying to impress someone. → **ROCK**

Having dinner with my parents

What do they want you to do?

- **ROCK** → This sounds like a trick. →
- **LAW** → What did you expect? → **CHANGE THE SUBJECT.**

SHOULD
I GET
THIS STREET
FOOD?

IS IT FOOD LITERALLY ON THE STREET?

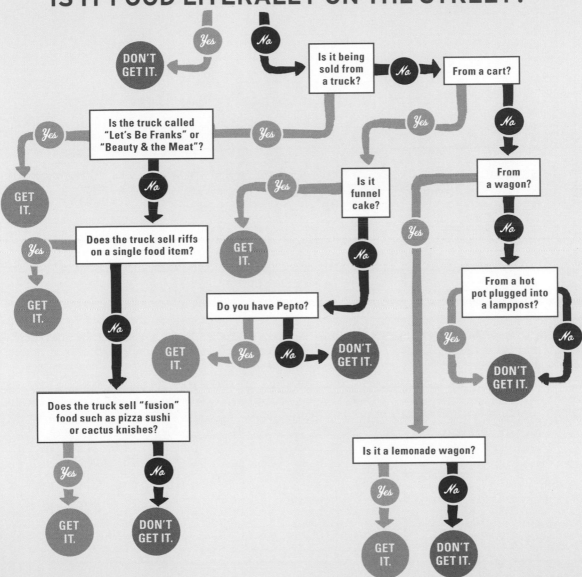

SHOULD I COMPETE IN THIS IRONMAN TRIATHLON?

HAVE YOU LOST YOUR MIND?

YES

NO

No kidding.

That's what you think.

SHOULD
I DO
LAUNDRY?

ARE YOU AN ADULT?

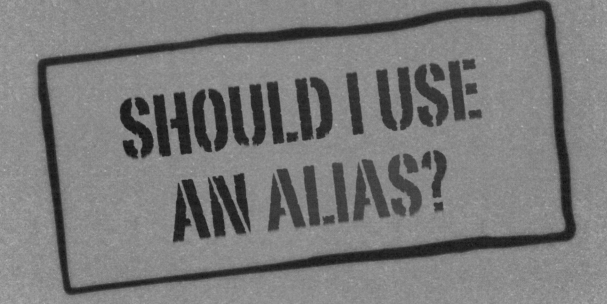

SHOULD I USE AN ALIAS?

CAN
I CALL IN
SICK?

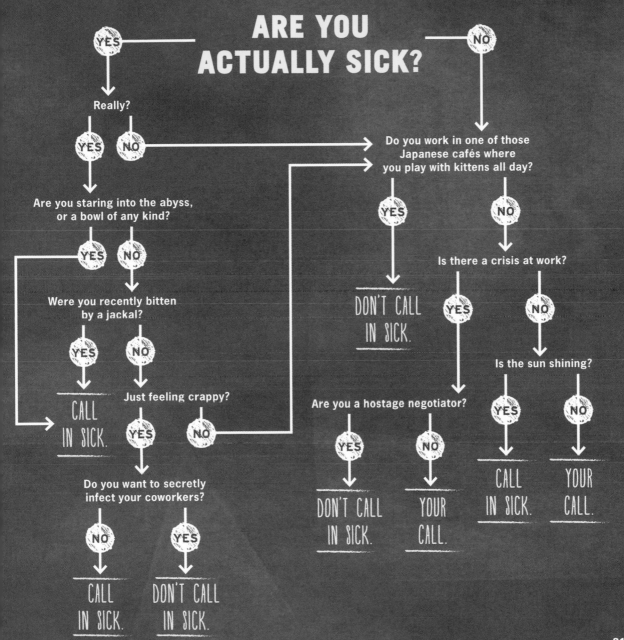

Can I

PARK HERE?

I just saw someone I know.

DO I SAY HI?

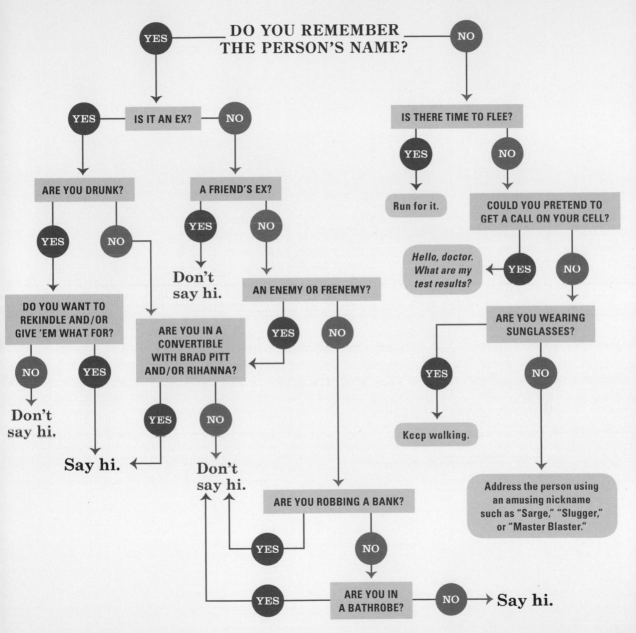

SHOULD I POST THIS ONLINE?

IS IT FUNNY?

37

CAN i WEAR A BINDI?

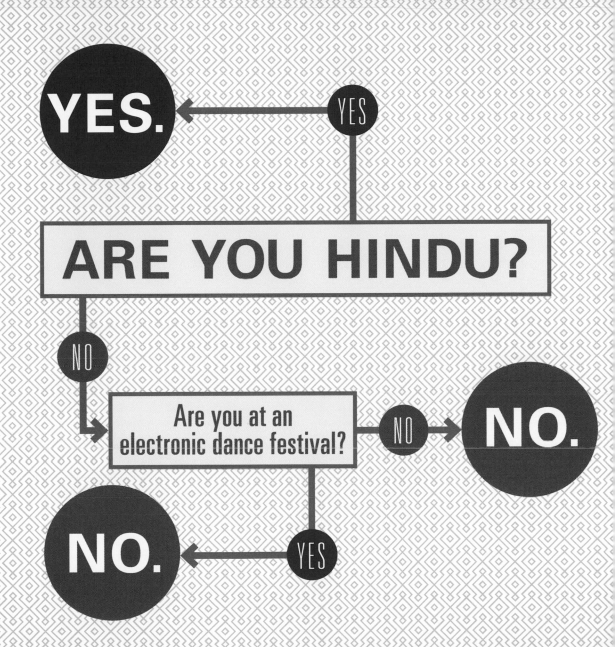

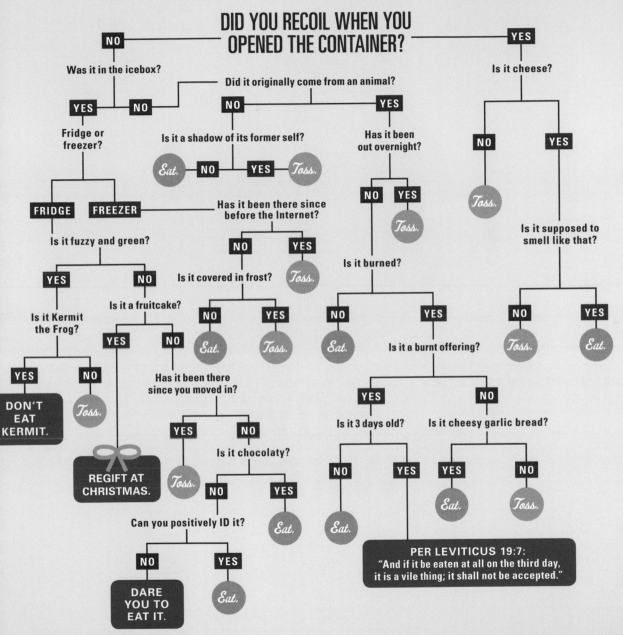

DID YOU RECOIL WHEN YOU OPENED THE CONTAINER?

NO ———— **YES**

NO branch

Was it in the icebox?

YES — **NO**

Did it originally come from an animal?

Fridge or freezer? (YES)

FRIDGE — **FREEZER**

FRIDGE
Is it fuzzy and green?

YES — **NO**

YES: Is it Kermit the Frog?
- **YES** → DON'T EAT KERMIT.
- **NO** → Toss.

NO: Is it a fruitcake?
- **YES** → REGIFT AT CHRISTMAS.
- **NO:** Has it been there since you moved in?
  - **YES** → Toss.
  - **NO:** Is it chocolaty?
    - **NO:** Can you positively ID it?
      - **NO** → DARE YOU TO EAT IT.
      - **YES** → Eat.
    - **YES** → Eat.

FREEZER
Has it been there since before the Internet?

NO — **YES**

NO: Is it covered in frost?
- **NO** → Eat.
- **YES** → Toss.

YES → Toss.

Did it originally come from an animal? (NO)

Is it a shadow of its former self?

Eat. — **NO** — **YES** — Toss.

Did it originally come from an animal? (YES)

Has it been out overnight?

NO — **YES** → Toss.

NO: Is it burned?
- **NO** → Eat.
- **YES:** Is it a burnt offering?
  - **YES:** Is it 3 days old?
    - **NO** → Eat.
    - **YES** →
      PER LEVITICUS 19:7:
      "And if it be eaten at all on the third day, it is a vile thing; it shall not be accepted."
  - **NO:** Is it cheesy garlic bread?
    - **YES** → Eat.
    - **NO** → Toss.

YES branch

Is it cheese?

NO → Toss.

YES: Is it supposed to smell like that?
- **NO** → Toss.
- **YES** → Eat.

I'M AT THE GYM.

NOW WHAT?

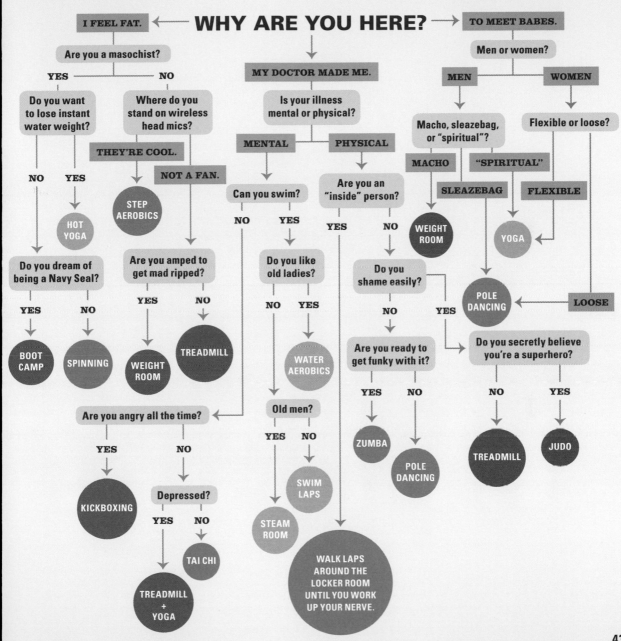

WHY ARE YOU HERE?

I FEEL FAT.

Are you a masochist?
- YES
- NO

YES → Do you want to lose instant water weight?
- NO
- YES → HOT YOGA

NO → Where do you stand on wireless head mics?
- THEY'RE COOL. → STEP AEROBICS
- NOT A FAN. → Are you amped to get mad ripped?

Do you dream of being a Navy Seal?
- YES → BOOT CAMP
- NO → SPINNING

Are you amped to get mad ripped?
- YES → WEIGHT ROOM
- NO → TREADMILL

Are you angry all the time?
- YES → KICKBOXING
- NO → Depressed?
  - YES → TREADMILL + YOGA
  - NO → TAI CHI

MY DOCTOR MADE ME.

Is your illness mental or physical?

MENTAL → Can you swim?
- NO → Are you angry all the time?
- YES → Do you like old ladies?
  - NO → Old men?
    - YES → STEAM ROOM
    - NO → SWIM LAPS
  - YES → WATER AEROBICS

PHYSICAL → Are you an "inside" person?
- YES → Do you shame easily?
  - NO → Are you ready to get funky with it?
    - YES → ZUMBA
    - NO → POLE DANCING
  - YES → POLE DANCING
- NO → WALK LAPS AROUND THE LOCKER ROOM UNTIL YOU WORK UP YOUR NERVE.

TO MEET BABES.

Men or women?

MEN → Macho, sleazebag, or "spiritual"?
- MACHO → WEIGHT ROOM
- SLEAZEBAG → POLE DANCING
- "SPIRITUAL" → YOGA

WOMEN → Flexible or loose?
- FLEXIBLE → YOGA
- LOOSE → POLE DANCING

Do you secretly believe you're a superhero?
- NO → TREADMILL
- YES → JUDO

Should I

CUT
MY HAIR?

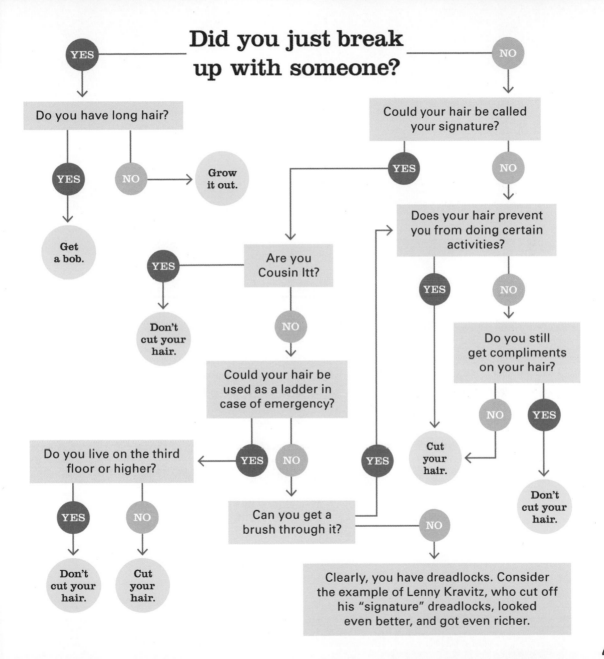

Did you just break up with someone?

YES → Do you have long hair?

- **YES** → Get a bob.
- **NO** → Grow it out.

NO → Could your hair be called your signature?

YES → Does your hair prevent you from doing certain activities?

- **YES** → Cut your hair.
- **NO** → Do you still get compliments on your hair?
  - **NO** → Cut your hair.
  - **YES** → Don't cut your hair.

Are you Cousin Itt?

- **YES** → Don't cut your hair.
- **NO** → Could your hair be used as a ladder in case of emergency?
  - **YES** → Do you live on the third floor or higher?
    - **YES** → Don't cut your hair.
    - **NO** → Cut your hair.
  - **NO** → Can you get a brush through it?
    - **YES** → Does your hair prevent you from doing certain activities?
    - **NO** → Clearly, you have dreadlocks. Consider the example of Lenny Kravitz, who cut off his "signature" dreadlocks, looked even better, and got even richer.

45

— Can I Wear —

THIS
SHIRT
IN PUBLIC?

IS IT VISIBLY STAINED?

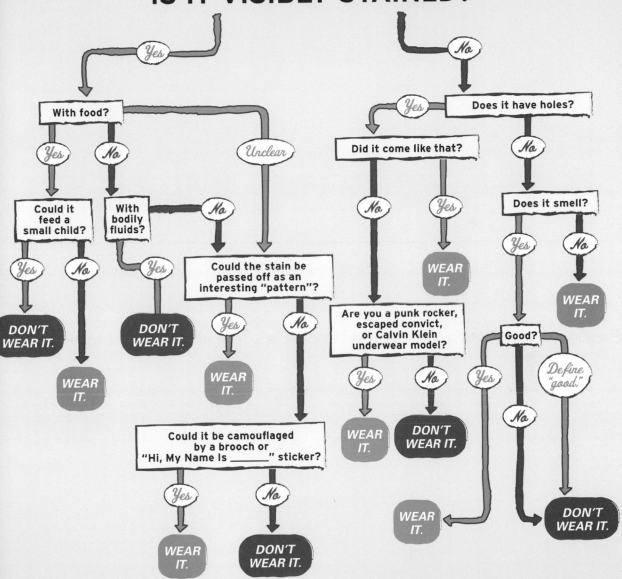

BLESS YOU

OR

GESUNDHEIT?

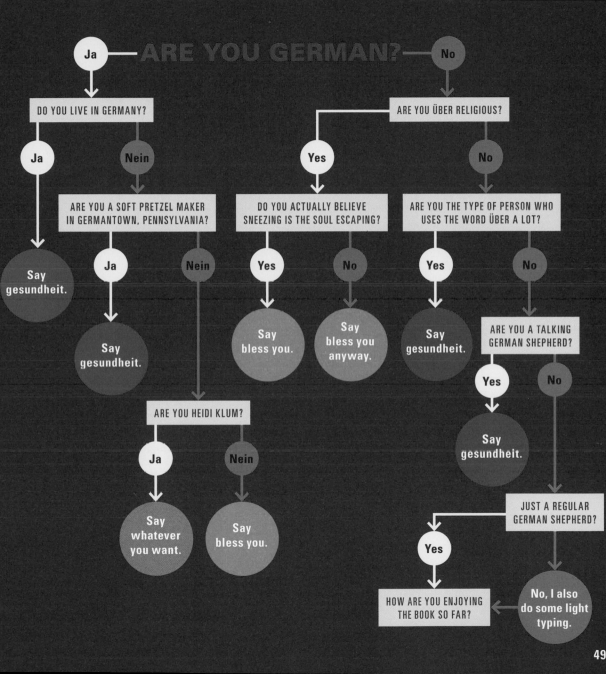

49

WHAT SHOULD I BE FOR HALLOWEEN?

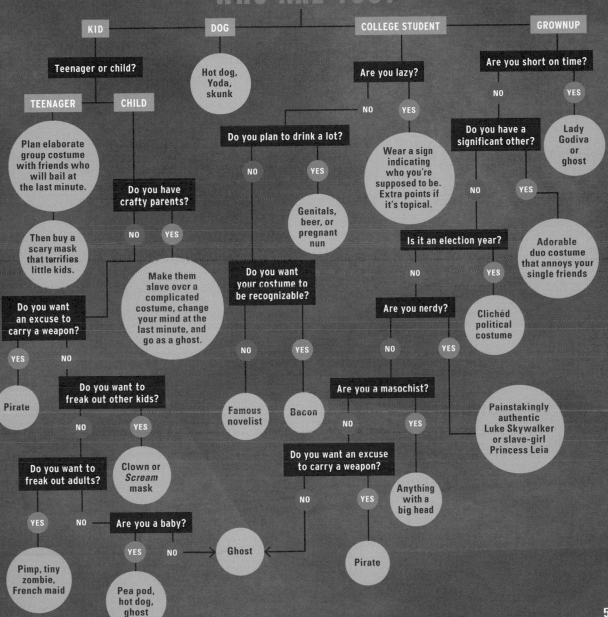

WHO ARE YOU?

KID — **DOG** — **COLLEGE STUDENT** — **GROWNUP**

Teenager or child?

DOG: Hot dog, Yoda, skunk

Are you lazy?

Are you short on time?

TEENAGER — **CHILD**

TEENAGER: Plan elaborate group costume with friends who will bail at the last minute.

Then buy a scary mask that terrifies little kids.

Do you have crafty parents?

Do you plan to drink a lot?

Are you lazy? YES: Wear a sign indicating who you're supposed to be. Extra points if it's topical.

Do you have a significant other?

Are you short on time? YES: Lady Godiva or ghost

Do you want an excuse to carry a weapon?

NO / **YES** (crafty parents)

Make them slave over a complicated costume, change your mind at the last minute, and go as a ghost.

Do you plan to drink a lot? YES: Genitals, beer, or pregnant nun

Do you want your costume to be recognizable?

Is it an election year?

Do you have a significant other? YES: Adorable duo costume that annoys your single friends

Do you want an excuse to carry a weapon? YES: Pirate

NO: Do you want to freak out other kids?

Are you nerdy?

Is it an election year? YES: Clichéd political costume

Do you want your costume to be recognizable? NO: Famous novelist

Do you want your costume to be recognizable? YES: Bacon

Are you a masochist?

Painstakingly authentic Luke Skywalker or slave-girl Princess Leia

Do you want to freak out other kids? NO: Do you want to freak out adults?

Do you want to freak out other kids? YES: Clown or *Scream* mask

Are you a masochist? NO: Do you want an excuse to carry a weapon?

Are you a masochist? YES: Anything with a big head

Do you want to freak out adults? YES: Pimp, tiny zombie, French maid

Do you want to freak out adults? NO: Are you a baby?

Ghost

Do you want an excuse to carry a weapon? YES: Pirate

Are you a baby? YES: Pea pod, hot dog, ghost

Are you a baby? NO: Ghost

51

SHOULD I GET THIS $15 SANDWICH?

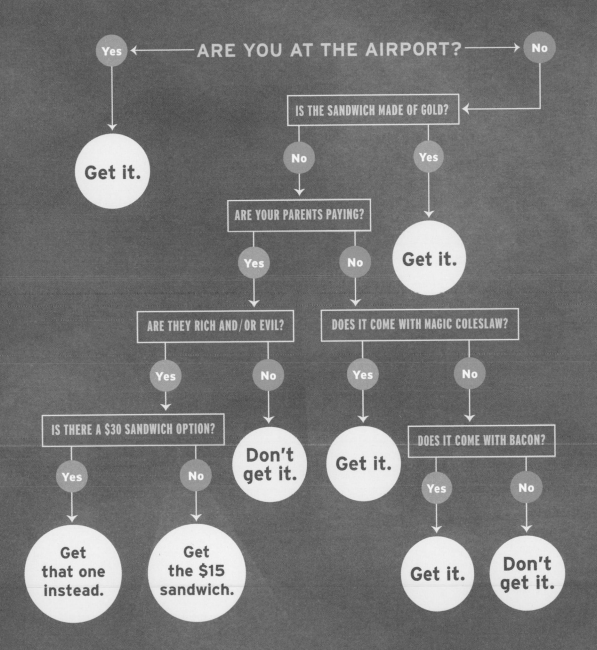

SHOULD I WATCH THIS PAULY SHORE MOVIE?

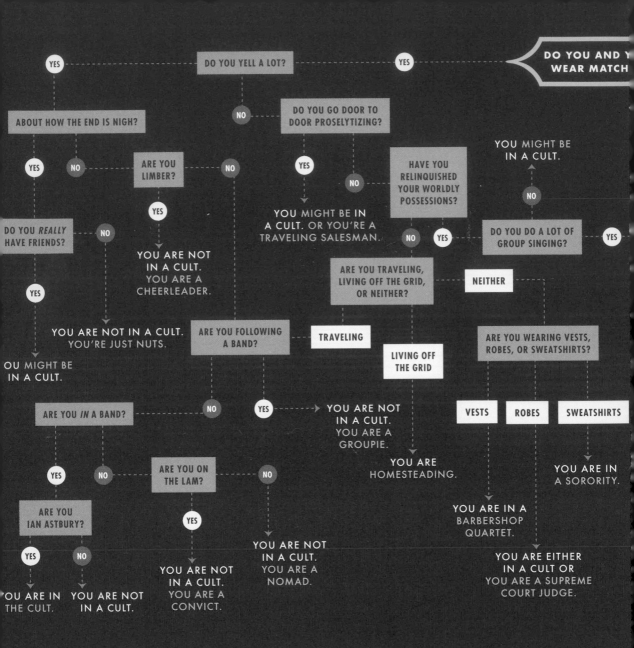

DO YOU AND Y[OU]
WEAR MATCH[...]

DO YOU YELL A LOT?

YES

YES

ABOUT HOW THE END IS NIGH?

NO

DO YOU GO DOOR TO
DOOR PROSELYTIZING?

YES

YES

NO

ARE YOU
LIMBER?

NO

YES

YES

HAVE YOU
RELINQUISHED
YOUR WORLDLY
POSSESSIONS?

YOU MIGHT BE
IN A CULT.

NO

DO YOU *REALLY*
HAVE FRIENDS?

NO

YES

YOU ARE NOT
IN A CULT.
YOU ARE A
CHEERLEADER.

YOU MIGHT BE IN
A CULT. OR YOU'RE A
TRAVELING SALESMAN.

NO

YES

DO YOU DO A LOT OF
GROUP SINGING?

YES

YES

ARE YOU TRAVELING,
LIVING OFF THE GRID,
OR NEITHER?

NEITHER

YOU ARE NOT IN A CULT.
YOU'RE JUST NUTS.

ARE YOU FOLLOWING
A BAND?

TRAVELING

ARE YOU WEARING VESTS,
ROBES, OR SWEATSHIRTS?

[Y]OU MIGHT BE
IN A CULT.

LIVING OFF
THE GRID

ARE YOU *IN* A BAND?

NO

YES

YOU ARE NOT
IN A CULT.
YOU ARE A
GROUPIE.

VESTS

ROBES

SWEATSHIRTS

YES

NO

ARE YOU ON
THE LAM?

NO

YOU ARE
HOMESTEADING.

YOU ARE IN
A SORORITY.

ARE YOU
IAN ASTBURY?

YES

YES

NO

YOU ARE NOT
IN A CULT.
YOU ARE A
NOMAD.

YOU ARE IN A
BARBERSHOP
QUARTET.

YES

NO

YOU ARE NOT
IN A CULT.
YOU ARE A
CONVICT.

YOU ARE EITHER
IN A CULT OR
YOU ARE A SUPREME
COURT JUDGE.

[Y]OU ARE IN
THE CULT.

YOU ARE NOT
IN A CULT.

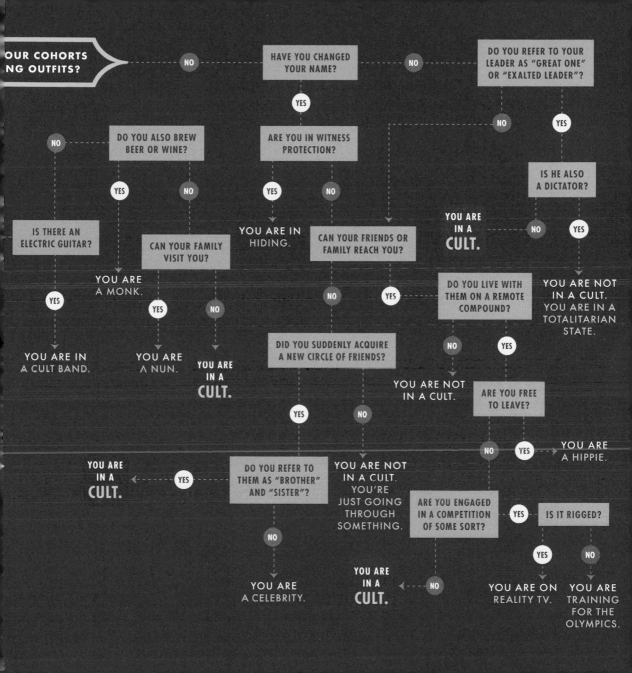

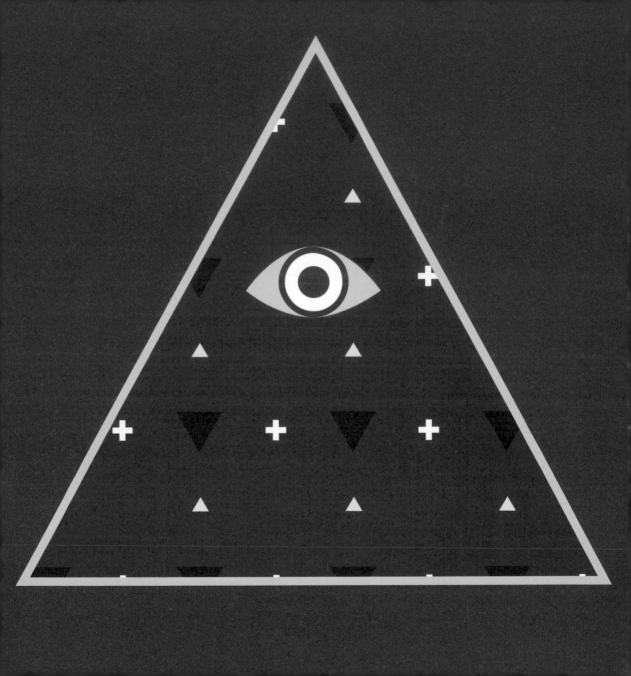

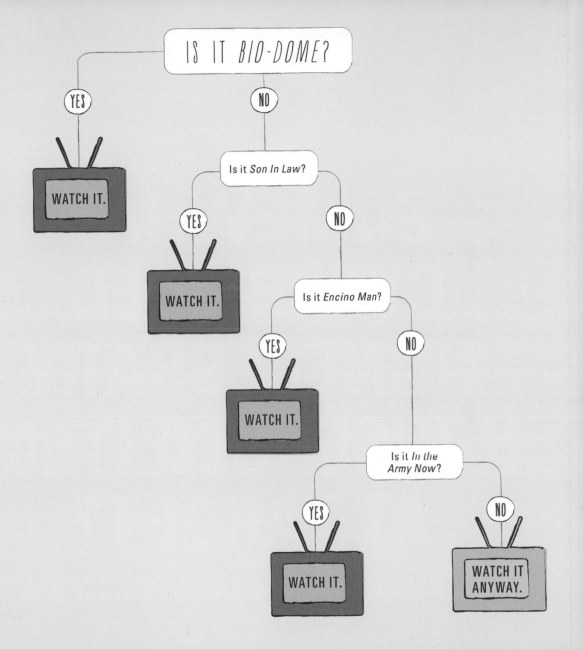

SOMEWHAT OVERPRICED, UNNECESSARY HOUSEHOLD ITEM AT TARGET?

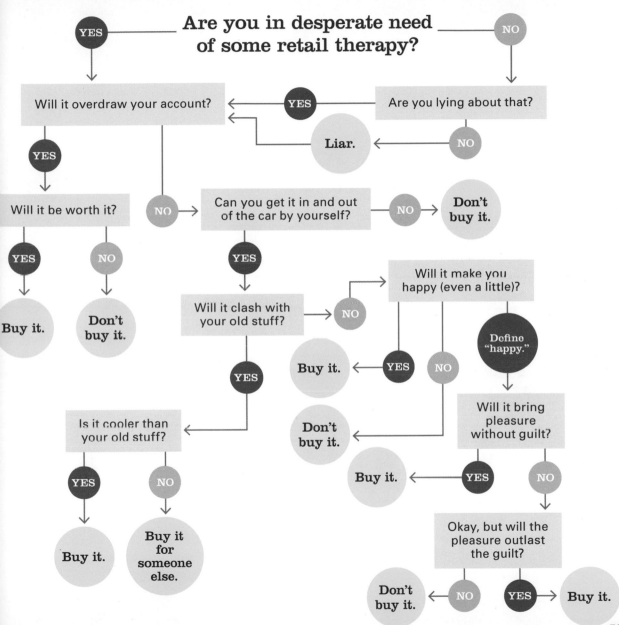

Are you in desperate need of some retail therapy?

YES → Will it overdraw your account?

NO → Are you lying about that?
- YES → Will it overdraw your account?
- NO → Liar. → Will it overdraw your account?

Will it overdraw your account?
- YES → Will it be worth it?
  - YES → Buy it.
  - NO → Don't buy it.
- NO → Can you get it in and out of the car by yourself?
  - NO → Don't buy it.
  - YES → Will it clash with your old stuff?
    - NO → Will it make you happy (even a little)?
      - YES → Buy it.
      - NO → Don't buy it.
      - Define "happy." → Will it bring pleasure without guilt?
        - YES → Buy it.
        - NO → Okay, but will the pleasure outlast the guilt?
          - NO → Don't buy it.
          - YES → Buy it.
    - YES → Is it cooler than your old stuff?
      - YES → Buy it.
      - NO → Buy it for someone else.

Shall
I get this
tattoo?

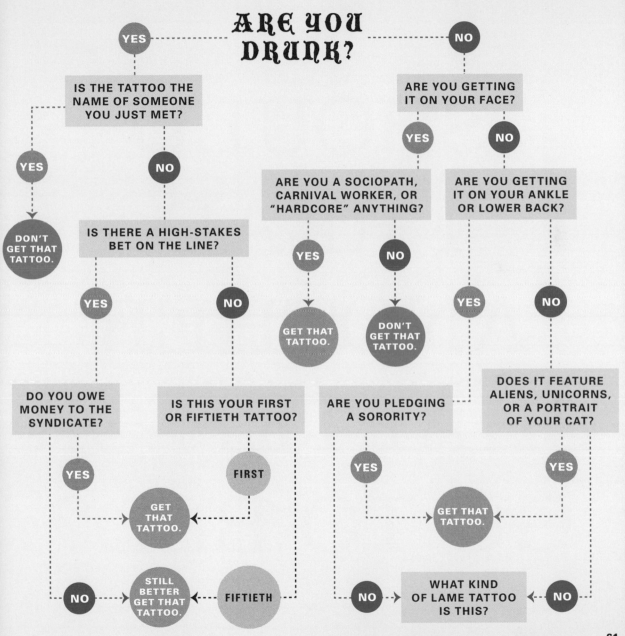

ARE YOU DRUNK?

YES — IS THE TATTOO THE NAME OF SOMEONE YOU JUST MET?

YES — DON'T GET THAT TATTOO.

NO — IS THERE A HIGH-STAKES BET ON THE LINE?

YES — DO YOU OWE MONEY TO THE SYNDICATE?

YES — GET THAT TATTOO.

NO — STILL BETTER GET THAT TATTOO.

NO — IS THIS YOUR FIRST OR FIFTIETH TATTOO?

FIRST — GET THAT TATTOO.

FIFTIETH — STILL BETTER GET THAT TATTOO.

NO — ARE YOU GETTING IT ON YOUR FACE?

YES — ARE YOU A SOCIOPATH, CARNIVAL WORKER, OR "HARDCORE" ANYTHING?

YES — GET THAT TATTOO.

NO — DON'T GET THAT TATTOO.

NO — ARE YOU GETTING IT ON YOUR ANKLE OR LOWER BACK?

YES — ARE YOU PLEDGING A SORORITY?

YES — GET THAT TATTOO.

NO — WHAT KIND OF LAME TATTOO IS THIS?

NO — DOES IT FEATURE ALIENS, UNICORNS, OR A PORTRAIT OF YOUR CAT?

YES — GET THAT TATTOO.

NO — WHAT KIND OF LAME TATTOO IS THIS?

61

SHOULD I READ ANOTHER CHAPTER OR GO TO BED?

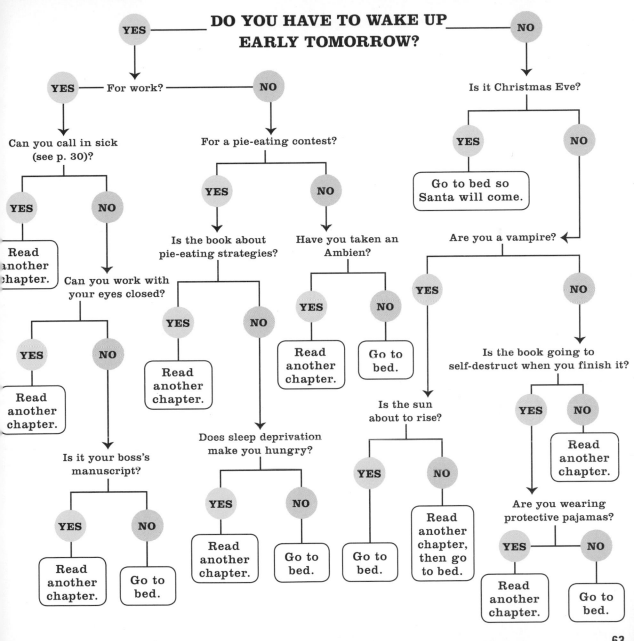

DO YOU HAVE TO WAKE UP EARLY TOMORROW?

YES ─── **NO**

YES ─── For work? ─── **NO**

Can you call in sick
(see p. 30)?

YES   **NO**

Read another chapter.

Can you work with
your eyes closed?

YES   **NO**

Read another chapter.

Is it your boss's
manuscript?

YES   **NO**

Read another chapter.

Go to bed.

For a pie-eating contest?

YES   **NO**

Is the book about
pie-eating strategies?

YES   **NO**

Read another chapter.

Does sleep deprivation
make you hungry?

YES   **NO**

Read another chapter.

Go to bed.

Have you taken an
Ambien?

YES   **NO**

Read another chapter.

Go to bed.

Is it Christmas Eve?

YES   **NO**

Go to bed so
Santa will come.

Are you a vampire?

YES   **NO**

Is the sun
about to rise?

YES   **NO**

Go to bed.

Read another chapter, then go to bed.

Is the book going to
self-destruct when you finish it?

YES   **NO**

Read another chapter.

Are you wearing
protective pajamas?

YES   **NO**

Read another chapter.

Go to bed.

63

SHOULD I CHANGE THE CHANNEL?

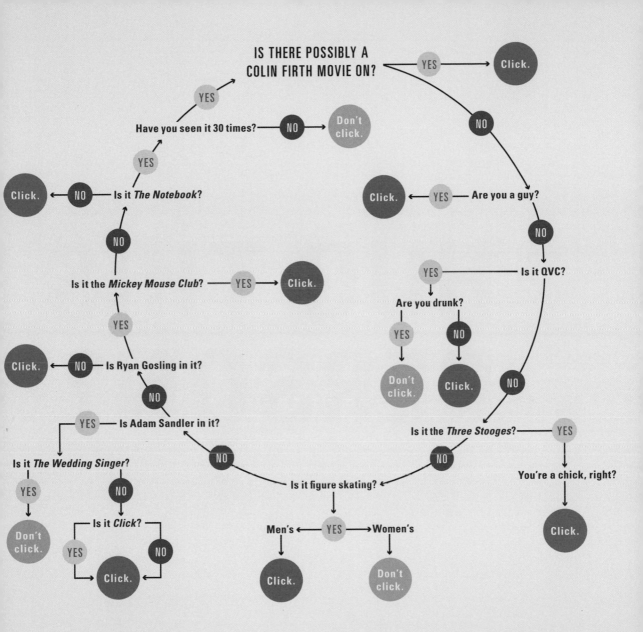

IS THERE POSSIBLY A COLIN FIRTH MOVIE ON?

YES → Click.

NO

Have you seen it 30 times? → NO → Don't click.

YES

Is it *The Notebook*? — NO → Click.

YES

Is it the *Mickey Mouse Club*? → YES → Click.

NO

Is Ryan Gosling in it? — NO → Click.

YES

Is Adam Sandler in it? — YES → Is it *The Wedding Singer*?

NO

Is it *The Wedding Singer*? → YES → Don't click.

NO → Is it *Click*? — YES → Click.

Is it *Click*? — NO → Click.

Are you a guy? — YES → Click.

NO

Is it QVC? — YES → Are you drunk?

Are you drunk? — YES → Don't click.

NO → Click.

Is it the *Three Stooges*? — YES → You're a chick, right? → Click.

NO

Is it figure skating? — YES → Men's → Click.

Women's → Don't click.

65

DO I HUG THIS PERSON?

SHOULD

I FINISH THIS
CARTON OF
ICE CREAM?

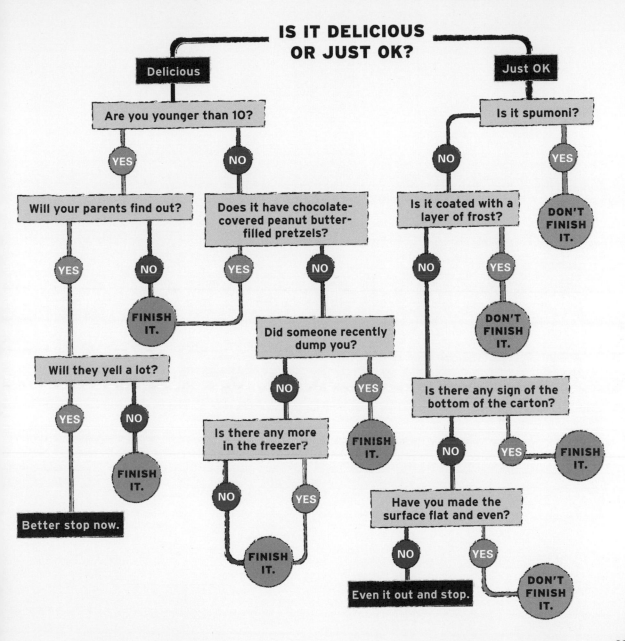

IS IT DELICIOUS OR JUST OK?

Delicious

Just OK

Are you younger than 10?

Is it spumoni?

YES → Will your parents find out?

NO → Does it have chocolate-covered peanut butter-filled pretzels?

NO → Is it coated with a layer of frost?

YES → **DON'T FINISH IT.**

YES → Will they yell a lot?

NO → **FINISH IT.**

YES → **FINISH IT.**

NO → Did someone recently dump you?

NO → Is it coated with a layer of frost?

YES → **DON'T FINISH IT.**

NO → Is there any sign of the bottom of the carton?

YES → Will they yell a lot?

NO → **FINISH IT.**

NO → Did someone recently dump you?

NO → Is there any more in the freezer?

YES → **FINISH IT.**

YES → Will they yell a lot?

YES → **Better stop now.**

NO → **FINISH IT.**

YES → **FINISH IT.**

Is there any more in the freezer?

NO → **FINISH IT.**

YES → **FINISH IT.**

Is there any sign of the bottom of the carton?

NO → Have you made the surface flat and even?

YES → **FINISH IT.**

Have you made the surface flat and even?

NO → **Even it out and stop.**

YES → **DON'T FINISH IT.**

Should I take an umbrella?

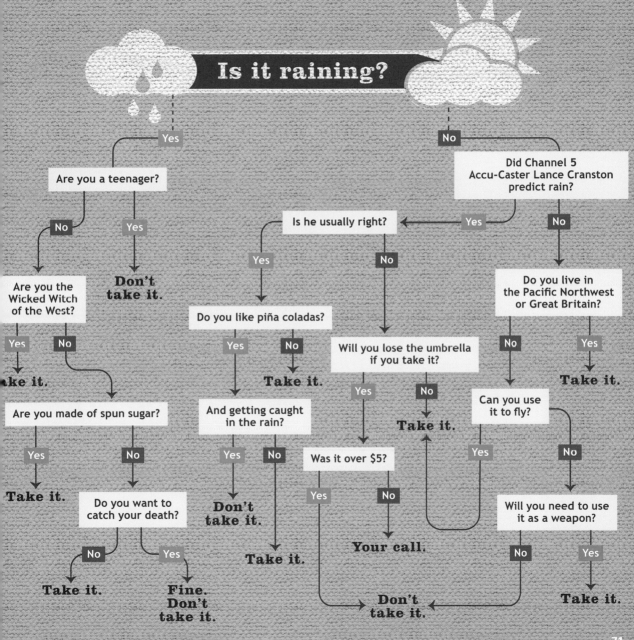

Is it raining?

Yes → Are you a teenager?

No → Are you the Wicked Witch of the West?

Yes → Take it.

No → Are you made of spun sugar?

Yes → Take it.

No → Do you want to catch your death?

No → Take it.

Yes → Fine. Don't take it.

Yes → Don't take it.

No → Did Channel 5 Accu-Caster Lance Cranston predict rain?

Yes → Is he usually right?

Yes → Do you like piña coladas?

Yes → And getting caught in the rain?

Yes → Don't take it.

No → Take it.

No → Take it.

No → Will you lose the umbrella if you take it?

Yes → Was it over $5?

Yes → Don't take it.

No → Take it.

No → Take it.

No → Do you live in the Pacific Northwest or Great Britain?

No → Can you use it to fly?

Yes → Your call.

No → Will you need to use it as a weapon?

No → Take it.

Yes → Take it.

Yes → Take it.

SHOULD I CLEAN UP AFTER MY DOG?

ARE YOU A BARBARIAN?

NO

Clean it up.

YES

Clean it up, please.

SHOTS

or

SODA WATER?

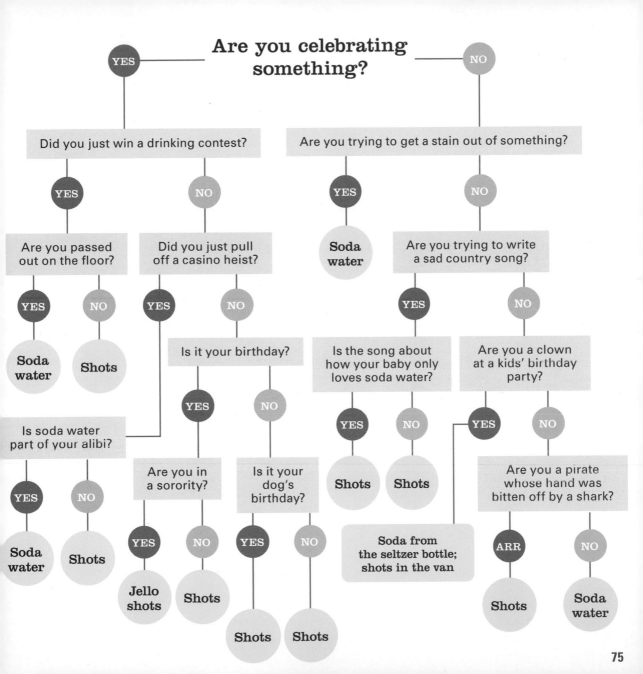

Are you celebrating something?

YES → Did you just win a drinking contest?

- YES → Are you passed out on the floor?
  - YES → **Soda water**
  - NO → **Shots**
- NO → Did you just pull off a casino heist?
  - YES → Is soda water part of your alibi?
    - YES → **Soda water**
    - NO → **Shots**
  - NO → Is it your birthday?
    - YES → Are you in a sorority?
      - YES → **Jello shots**
      - NO → **Shots**
    - NO → Is it your dog's birthday?
      - YES → **Shots**
      - NO → **Shots**

NO → Are you trying to get a stain out of something?

- YES → **Soda water**
- NO → Are you trying to write a sad country song?
  - YES → Is the song about how your baby only loves soda water?
    - YES → **Shots**
    - NO → **Shots**
  - NO → Are you a clown at a kids' birthday party?
    - YES → **Soda from the seltzer bottle; shots in the van**
    - NO → Are you a pirate whose hand was bitten off by a shark?
      - ARR → **Shots**
      - NO → **Soda water**

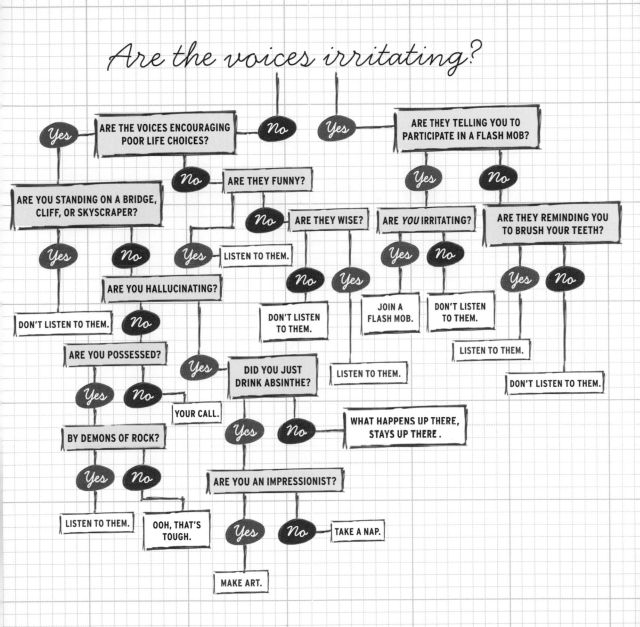

Should I Hit SNOOZE AGAIN?

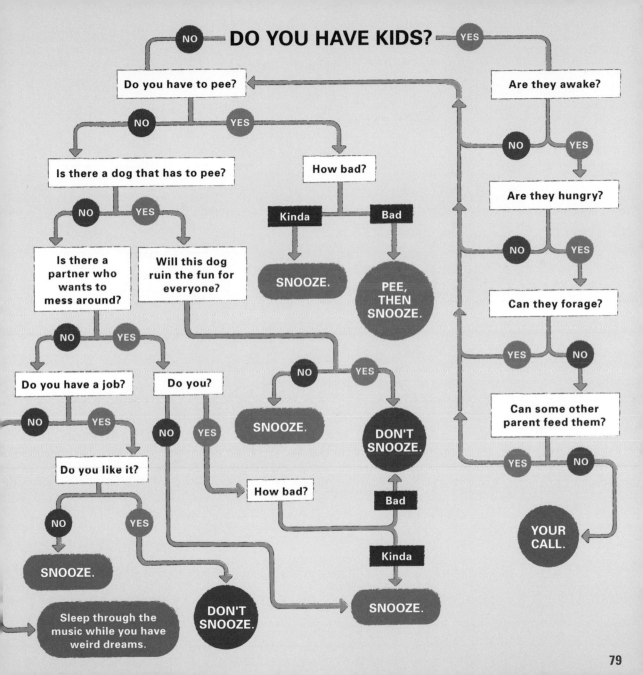

79

SHOULD I SEND FLOWERS?

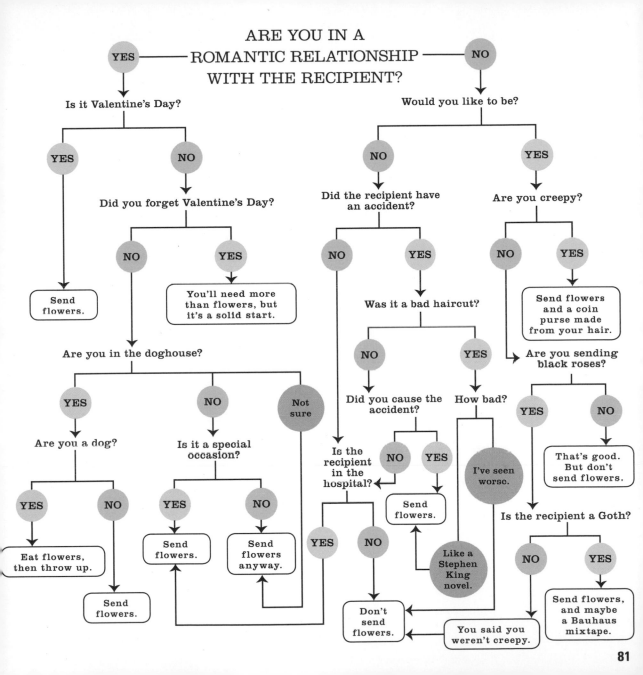

ARE YOU IN A ROMANTIC RELATIONSHIP WITH THE RECIPIENT?

YES — Is it Valentine's Day?
- YES → Send flowers.
- NO → Did you forget Valentine's Day?
  - YES → You'll need more than flowers, but it's a solid start.
  - NO → Are you in the doghouse?
    - YES → Are you a dog?
      - YES → Eat flowers, then throw up.
      - NO → Send flowers.
    - NO → Is it a special occasion?
      - YES → Send flowers.
      - NO → Send flowers anyway.
    - Not sure

NO — Would you like to be?
- NO → Did the recipient have an accident?
  - NO → Is the recipient in the hospital?
    - YES → Send flowers.
    - NO → Don't send flowers.
  - YES → Was it a bad haircut?
    - NO → Did you cause the accident?
      - NO
      - YES → Send flowers.
    - YES → How bad?
      - I've seen worse.
      - Like a Stephen King novel.
- YES → Are you creepy?
  - NO → Send flowers and a coin purse made from your hair.
  - YES → Are you sending black roses?
    - YES → Is the recipient a Goth?
      - NO → You said you weren't creepy.
      - YES → Send flowers, and maybe a Bauhaus mixtape.
    - NO → That's good. But don't send flowers.

81

What Should I Do

WITH THIS

EMPTY
BOTTLE?

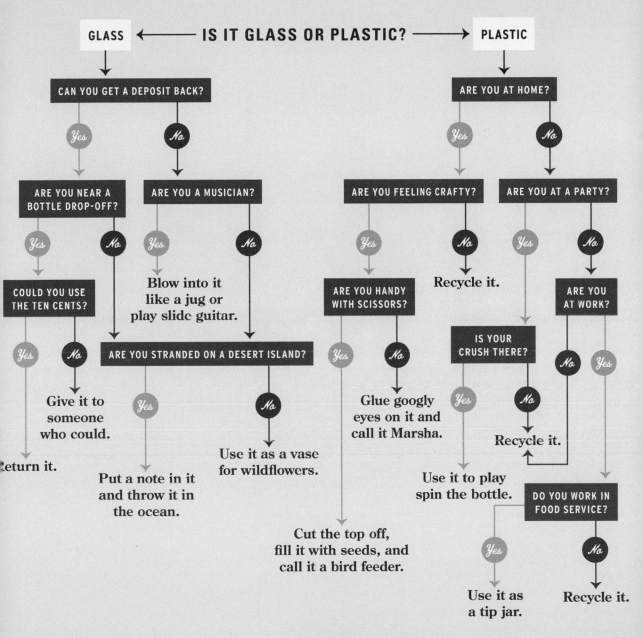

SHOULD I WEAR THIS WEAR THIS FEDORA?

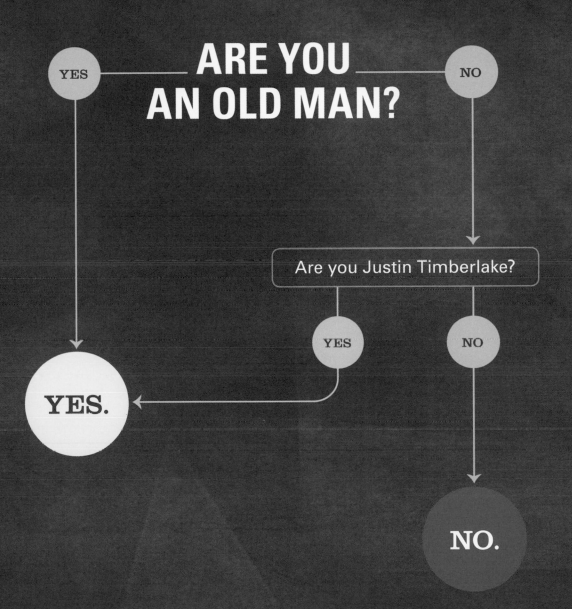

Should I

SQUISH THIS BUG?

SHOULD I CALL MY PARENTS?

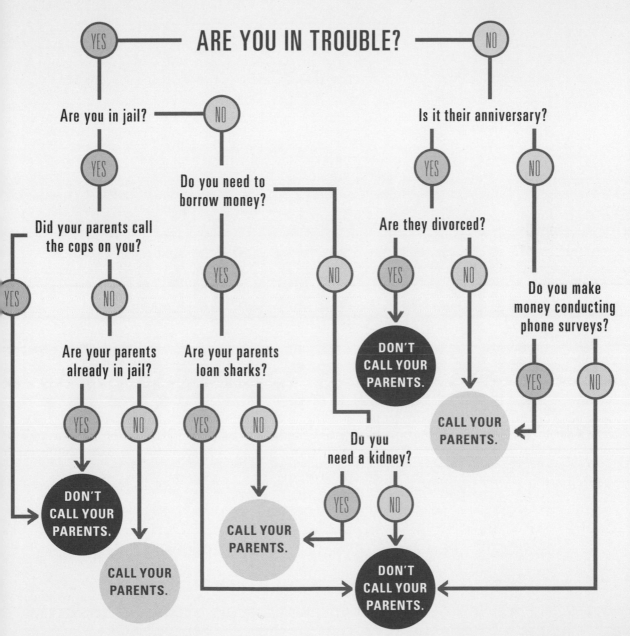

ARE YOU IN TROUBLE?

HOW SHOULD I PROCRASTINATE?

WHAT ARE YOU PUTTING OFF?

WORK

Have you organized your desk drawers?

YES / **NO** → Do that.

Have you cleaned up your computer desktop lately?

YES / **NO** → Do that.

Have you Googled "[your name] is hot"?

YES / **NO** → Do that.

Have you wiped down all flat surfaces?

YES / **NO** → Do that.

Have you taken out the trash?

YES / **NO** → Do that.

Take a nap in a utility closet.

HOUSEWORK

Have you worked out?

YES / **NO** → Do that.

Do you have a Bedazzler?

NO / **YES** → Bedazzle stuff.

Do you have a partner?

NO / **YES** → Start a fight.

Do you have a pet?

NO / **YES** → Make clothes for it.

Do you have a blog?

NO → Start one. / **YES** → Take the Mensa test, then blog about it.

WORKING OUT

Do you have any work stuff to do?

NO / **YES** → Do it.

Are your books alphabetized?

YES / **NO** → Do that.

Do you have a DVR?

NO / **YES** → Delete stuff you're never going to watch.

Can you name all 50 states in alphabetical order?

YES / **NO** → Learn.

In under 30 seconds?

YES → Memorize the state birds. / **NO** → Learn.

SHOULD I HAVE SEX TONIGHT?

ARE YOU A GUY OR GIRL?

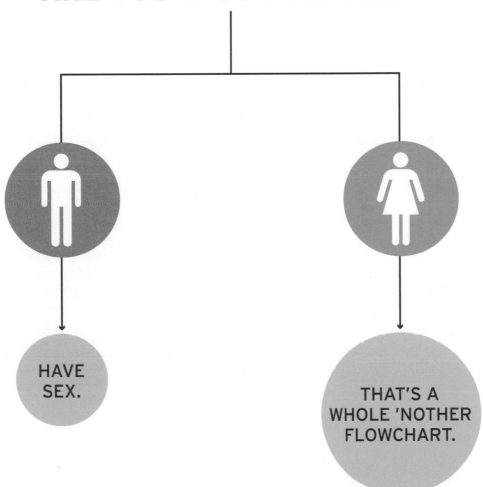

HAVE SEX.

THAT'S A WHOLE 'NOTHER FLOWCHART.

IS THIS SONG

KARAOKE-WORTHY?

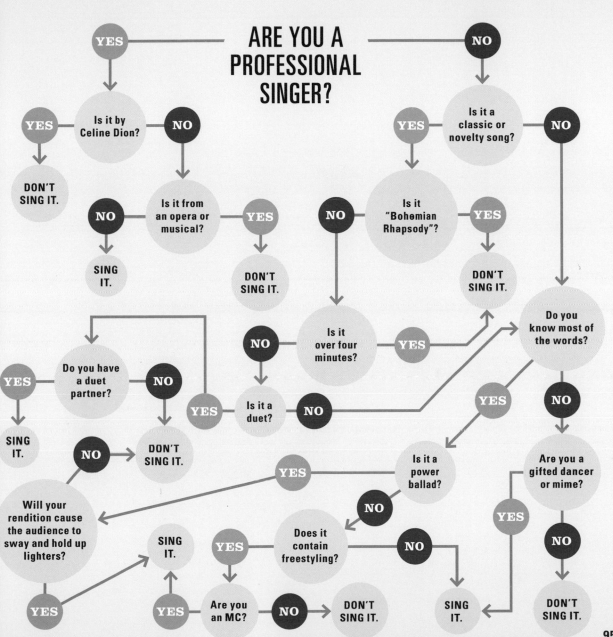